Contents

Christmas 4

Felt stocking 6

Sleigh sweetie dish 8

Paper ribbon wreath 10

Toilet roll tube reindeer 12

Pine cone elf 14

Santa tree decoration 16

Candy cane Christmas card 18

Christmas tree advent calendar ... 20

Rocking robin bauble 22

Glossary and Index 24

D0417414

Christmas

There is no better time to get crafty than at Christmas. You can use the projects in this book to make special, handmade gifts for your friends and family, or to create festive decorations. Each craft will take you only about 10 minutes, but don't feel the need to rush! You can build up some festive excitement by making and creating your way through December!

Elf: pages 14–15

Christmas is a great time to recycle, too. There will be lots of things that you might otherwise throw away that make great craft materials. Before you chuck it, check it! Can any packaging or boxes be flattened into pieces of card that you could use to make the stocking templates on pages 6–7? Is there any leftover Christmas wrapping paper that you can use to decorate the wreath on pages 10–11? Or can you save bits of ribbons from crackers or presents to make the elf's present on pages 14–15? There are lots more possibilities, so if you think something may be useful, save it and keep it in a safe place ready for the next time you get creative.

Crafting can be messy, especially if you are using glitter or glues, so make sure you cover all your work surfaces with old newspaper or a plastic tablecloth before you begin. Always wash your hands after you have used glue to stop your works of art being ruined by sticky fingers, and always ask an adult to help you with scissors or sharp compasses.

Santa: pages 16–17

Robin: pages 22–23

So, put on a Christmas jumper, tuck into a mince pie and get messy!

5

Felt stocking

These mini stockings are perfect for storing tiny treats or candy canes. You could hang them on a Christmas tree or give them as a gift.

Watch this step-by-step video of the felt stocking being made!

1

Draw a stocking shape that is no bigger than 10cm x 10cm onto some card, and cut it out to make a template.

2

Cut two stocking shapes out of the red felt, using the card template as a guide.

3

Sew some strips of ribbon onto one of the stocking shapes.

4

Place one of the stocking shapes on top of the other, with the decoration facing outwards, and sew around the outside, leaving the top open.

5

Sew a strip of white felt around the top of the stocking. Finish by sewing a loop of ribbon and a button to the top of the stocking so you can hang it up.

To make the stocking extra special, personalize it by cutting a letter out of felt and sewing it on.

Sleigh sweetie dish

Dashing through the snow can be hungry work! Use this handy dish to serve up some Christmas treats.

You will need:
- Red card
- A pen
- An empty cream cheese container with a lid
- Scissors
- Sticky pads
- Two wide lolly sticks
- Red pipe cleaners
- Craft glue
- Paper fasteners
- Glitter glue

1

Draw two sleigh shapes onto some red card, making sure they are big enough to cover the long sides of your container.

2

Cut them out and stick them onto the container using sticky pads.

3

Cut some more card to cover the front and back of the container and attach it using sticky pads.

4

Stick the sleigh onto the lid with sticky pads, then stick all of this onto the two lolly sticks, using more sticky pads. Curl up some pipe cleaners to make the skis, and glue them onto the sticks.

5

Decorate the sides with paper fasteners and swirls of glitter glue and leave to dry completely before filling with sweets.

Make nine of the reindeer on pp12-13 and attach them to the sleigh using some sparkly string.

Display your cards in this pretty indoor wreath made from paper and card.

Watch this step-by-step video of the paper ribbon wreath being made!

You will need:
- A pair of compasses
- A ruler
- A pencil
- Corrugated card
- Scissors
- String
- Craft glue
- Assorted green paper
- A glue stick
- Red tissue paper

1

Use your compasses to draw a 20cm circle with a 10cm circle inside it onto the corrugated card to make a ring. Repeat, so you have two rings in total, and then cut both out.

2

Use the compasses to make a small hole at the top of one of the rings. Tie some string through this hole to make a loop.

3 Spread glue over one of the rings. Stick the two rings together, leaving the knot on the string on the outside.

4 Cut the green papers into 10cm x 3cm strips. Fold each strip in half lengthways, without making a crease, and start sticking them onto the ring.

5 Rip the tissue paper into small pieces and roll these into balls. Glue the balls around the ring in clusters of three.

No Christmas scene is complete without a reindeer or two. You could even try making all nine of Santa's reindeer: Dasher, Dancer, Prancer, Vixen, Comet, Cupid, Donner, Blitzen and, of course, Rudolf!

You will need:

- Two toilet roll tubes
- Brown paper
- Scissors
- A glue stick
- Brown pipe cleaners
- Sticky tape
- A stapler
- Craft glue
- Googly eyes
- White paper
- A brown bead

1

Cut some brown paper to fit around the tubes, and glue it in place.

2

Place two pipe cleaners inside one of the tubes and fix in place with sticky tape. Bend them to make legs, then bend up the ends to make feet so the reindeer can stand.

3

Cut the other brown tube in half, and staple one half onto the body. This will be the head. Shape the front with scissors to make a mouth.

4

Staple another two pipe cleaners to the top of the head and bend them into antler shapes.

5

Glue some googly eyes onto the face and make a tail from brown and white scrap paper. Glue a brown bead to the top of the head to make a nose.

Decorate the Christmas dinner table with a reindeer in each place, and write each person's name on the side to make seasonal place settings.

Pine cone elf

Getting some fresh air at Christmas can be fun after all that food! Next time you're out and about, try collecting some pine cones so you can make a team of Christmas elves to help Santa out!

You will need:
- Fabric glue
- A flesh-coloured pom-pom
- A pine cone
- Two googly eyes
- Two green pipe cleaners
- Scissors
- Green and red felt
- A small white pom-pom
- Red ribbon

1

Use the fabric glue to stick the flesh-coloured pom-pom to the top of the pine cone. Stick the two googly eyes onto the pom-pom.

2

Wrap one pipe cleaner around the top of the pine cone to make the arms and the other pipe cleaner around the bottom to make the legs. Bend up the bottom of the legs to make feet and make sure the elf can stand up straight.

3

Cut out a semicircle of green felt 5cm in diameter. Fold this into a cone shape and stick the edges together using fabric glue. Glue the small white pom-pom on the point and stick the hat to the head.

4

Cut out four mitten shapes from the red felt. Glue two mitten shapes to the end of each arm, sandwiching the pipe cleaners.

5

Decorate your elf with a red felt stripe around the hat, and a red zig-zag collar around the neck. You could also make a felt present with a red ribbon for the elf to hold in its arms.

Remember to always wash your winter finds before you start using them to make elves. When you are out, you may also find acorns and conkers. These are great to make mini elves with!

Santa tree decoration

This jolly Santa will Ho-Ho-Ho-pefully add some Christmas cheer to the top of your tree.

You will need:
- Scissors
- Red card
- A paper doily
- White paper
- Flesh-coloured paper
- A glue stick
- Green card
- A black marker pen
- A stapler
- Fabric glue
- A small, white pom-pom

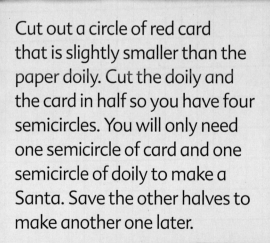

1

Cut out a circle of red card that is slightly smaller than the paper doily. Cut the doily and the card in half so you have four semicircles. You will only need one semicircle of card and one semicircle of doily to make a Santa. Save the other halves to make another one later.

2

Cut out a beard and moustache from white paper and a face shape from flesh-coloured paper. Stick them together with the glue stick. Cut some red arms and green mittens out of card, and stick them together, too.

3

Draw around the face and arms with the marker pen.

4

Glue the doily to the underneath of the red card semicircle, fold the whole thing up into a cone and staple into place.

5

Stick the face and arms onto the cone, and glue the white pom-pom to the top.

Make lots of Santas and peg them up in a long line to make Christmas bunting that you can hang from the ceiling or along a wall.

Everyone loves receiving a Christmas card, but this card is also a gift! Secretly store a delicious candy cane inside to send a little treat to someone special.

You will need:

- White A4 card
- A ruler
- A pen
- Scissors
- A candy cane
- Sticky tape
- Yellow and green card
- Craft glue
- Star and spot-shaped stickers

1

Fold your A4 card in half and make a firm crease.

2

With the card still folded, cut a 1cm slit in the fold that is 2cm from the bottom, and another one 5cm along to the right of it.

3 Open the card up and press the cut pieces inwards to make a long box shape. Be sure to press down firmly to make a good crease.

4 Turn the card upside down, and hook the curved part of the candy cane into the box. Secure it in place with sticky tape.

5 Turn the card the right way up, and transform the candy cane into a Christmas tree by cutting out a yellow star for the top and a green tree shape to stick to the back of the cane. Use the stickers to decorate the rest of the card.

The countdown to Christmas can begin with a homemade advent calendar that you can personalize and decorate.

You will need:
- A4 green card
- Scissors
- A ruler
- A pen
- Spot-shaped stickers
- Yellow and red card
- A glue stick

1

Cut the green card into a long triangle.

2

Starting 2cm from the bottom, draw and cut 12 slits, 2cm apart, on either side of the triangle, leaving a 1.5cm gap between them in the middle.

3

Write 1—24 on the end of the slits, starting from the bottom. Fold the end of each slit over by 1.5cm, leaving the bottom one unfolded. Write the matching number on the top of every flap.

4

Secure each flap down with a sticker. Fold the top of the tree down to make the 25th flap.

5

Cut the bottom slits of paper off to make a trunk. Stick a red bucket shape to the bottom of it and then make a star out of the yellow card to go on the top. Decorate the rest of the tree with more stickers.

Rocking ro in bauble

Turn a plain bauble into a fun, quirky character that will brighten up any Christmas tree.

You will need:
- Brown, yellow and red felt
- Scissors
- A bronze bauble
- Fabric glue
- Googly eyes
- An orange pipe cleaner
- Glitter glue

1

Cut out felt shapes to decorate your bauble. You will need two brown wings, a yellow beak made from two triangles, and a red circle.

2

Use the fabric glue to stick all the felt shapes to the bauble.

3

Add a googly eye to each side of the bauble, sticking in place using the fabric glue.

4

Bend a pipe cleaner into claw shapes and glue them to the bottom of the bauble.

Try decorating a silver bauble to look like a Christmas pudding, complete with felt holly leaves on top!

5

Add some sparkle by decorating the felt with glitter glue.

Glossary

antlers solid, bony growths on the head of a deer

bauble a round, coloured decoration hung on a Christmas tree

bunting a row of cloth or paper decorations on a string

doily a small napkin made of lace or lace-like paper

festive about a festival or a holiday

igloo a dome-shaped house made of blocks of ice and snow

seasonal something that happens only at a certain time of year

wreath a ring-shaped decoration

Index

advent calendar 20–21

bauble 21, 22–23

candy cane 6, 18–19

Christmas card 18–19

Christmas tree 6, 16, 19, 20–21, 22

elf 4, 14–15

gifts 4, 6, 15, 18

pine cones 14–15

reindeer 7, 12–13

robin 22–23

Santa 12, 14, 16–17

sleigh 8–9

stocking 4, 6–7

wreath 4, 10–11